SEATTLE

SEATTLE

PHOTOGRAPHY BY CHARLES KREBS

TEXT BY TIMOTHY EGAN

GRAPHIC ARTS CENTER PUBLISHING COMPANY • PORTLAND, OREGON

International Standard Book Number 1-55868-000-4 (Hardbound)
International Standard Book Number 1-55868-001-2 (Softbound)
Library of Congress Catalog Number 86-80096
© MCMLXXXVI by Graphic Arts Center Publishing Company
P.O. Box 10306 • Portland, Oregon 97210 • 503/226-2402
Editor-in-Chief • Douglas A. Pfeiffer
Designer • Robert Reynolds
Typographer • Paul O. Giesey/Adcrafters
Printer • Graphic Arts Center
Bindery • Lincoln & Allen
Printed in the United States of America
Revised Edition

■ *Frontispiece:* The muddy little village at the mouth of the Duwamish River is now a polished international port. Here, a summer breeze guides sailboats on Lake Union past downtown Seattle.

UNDER THE VOLCANO

At two thousand feet, the plane dropped below a ceiling of clouds riding a Pacific breeze, and the Seattle native turned to the visitor sitting next to him. He whispered a single word—home—and for the first time in years, he felt it. His friend, long bullied by the winds of Lake Erie, lived in Buffalo. The native was born on Queen Anne, an inner city slope crowded with urban charms, but he had been away so long he felt as if he were descending on a new land, a pocket of paradise with enough room to take in a prodigal son.

By the time they landed, his friend was reeling from visual overload: the glaciers of Mount Rainier, the islands of Puget Sound, the streams draining the west side of the Cascades into clear waters surrounded by almost a million people. Even then, the real surprise did not hit him until they drove into town. He could not take his eyes off the wind-shaped firs growing in roadside strips between the lanes of concrete.

"I don't believe this," he gushed. "Trees — right between the freeways — and nobody has tried to steal 'em yet."

Anyone who has ever lived in Seattle has a story about introducing a guest to the city. A first glance is like first love, unforgettable, perhaps a bit too romanticized. We tend to ignore the industrial jungle along the Duwamish and point instead to the local company with global reach, Boeing. We like the new buildings bumping against the low clouds downtown, but inevitably steer toward Seattle's first skyscraper, the Smith Tower. For nearly half a century, we point out, this landmark was the tallest building west of the Mississippi. We give in, after feigning disinterest, and take the visitor to Pike Place Market, called "the heart and soul of the city" by Mark Tobey, a native painter of world renown. And always, we have much to say about the punctuation mark on the southeastern skyline—Rainier.

The Indians, who remembered its violent past, mythologized it with the name "Tahoma," the mountain that is god. Captain George Vancouver, who sailed into Puget Sound in 1792 and renamed nearly everything of prominence after a friend, distant cousin, or superior back in England, was moved beyond his usual dry prose. He called the local environs and the 14,410-foot volcano "a landscape almost as enchantingly beautiful as the most elegant finished pleasure grounds of Europe." Two centuries later, Supreme Court Justice William O. Douglas remembered closing his eyes inside a New York subway and seeing the eternal snowfields of Rainier. As a boy, he had climbed its ridges and felt the cool breath of the mountain. First love.

Much of Seattle's geologic past also can be traced to the volcano. Ragged glaciers, not unlike those which now cover nearly thirty-five square miles of Rainier, retreated from the Puget Sound lowland during the end of the last Ice Age about ten thousand years ago. The woolly mammoth romped around the Sound, nibbling on grass at the edge of the ice walls. The glaciers carved out hills and flattened valleys and raised the water level of the Sound three hundred feet. Then, about five thousand years ago, the top part of Rainier's summit broke away, causing the massive Osceola Mudflow. This wall of wet earth, one of the largest which geologists have found, spread all the way to present-day Kent. The flow left a fertile valley, today a home base for truck farmers selling their produce at the Pike Place Market, and it left a continual reminder of Rainier's power.

There is considerable evidence that Native Americans were around when the last of the lowland ice melted away about 8,000 B.C. The artwork of numerous coast tribes suggests that, like latter-day residents of Seattle, they too felt blessed. The climate was kind and they lived well, building longhouses, dining on salmon, berries, and game. Supposedly, Chief Sealth of the Suquamish Tribe saw Vancouver's ship, the *Discovery,* sail into Puget Sound. Sealth was just a kid then, and more than half a century would go by before he saw another historic vessel. It was 1851 when the pioneer schooner, *Exact,* tied up at Alki Point, and twelve white adults and an equal number of children disembarked. Sealth welcomed the Arthur Denny party, told them about local food sources and quirks of the land, and watched them as they hacked four cabins out of the timber — unaware that within five years they would own his lifelong stomping grounds. Property ownership was a concept for which his tribe did not have a word.

Sealth made friends with Doc Maynard, a middle-aged midwesterner on the run from a bad marriage and given to excessive drinking. When a territorial clerk in Olympia asked the name of the settlement, which had just been relocated at the mouth of the Duwamish after one miserable winter at Alki, the name Duwamps was offered. Maynard, fortunately, suggested Seattle — after his friend the chief, whose name Sealth was difficult for the newcomers to pronounce.

From most accounts, the chief died horrified at the thought that so many whites would speak his name long after his death — and burden his spirit. But he left an eloquent last speech, its poetic intent undiminished by the apparent polish of the translator. "Our dead never forget the beautiful world that gave them being," said the old chief. "Every part of this soil is sacred in the estimation of my people. The very dust responds more lovingly to their footsteps than to yours, because it is rich with the dust of our ancestors."

One year after the town was named, Henry Yesler brought the muscle of a steam-powered sawmill to the struggling settlement. Seattle was carpeted with ancient firs, some as old as five hundred years and as tall as a fifteen-story building. The mill gobbled up timber that was scooted down the original skid road, and a booming log trade brought other settlers and a steady flow of ships to the deep, natural harbor at Elliott Bay. Many of the original pioneers were God-fearing working folk, but an equal number were not, and several historians contend that Seattle would not have become the premier city of the Northwest were it not for the first-rate bordello built next to Yesler's mill. Seattle's rowdy early history, a story of commerce and carnality, is well chronicled, particularly in Murray Morgan's timeless *Skid Road.*

One consistent theme emerging from a broad view of Seattle's history is the city's maverick streak. An aversion to conformity infused such diverse events as Arthur Denny's coup in obtaining a university from the territorial government in 1861, thirty years before anyone would have any use for it; the building of the Ship Canal in 1917; the opening of Bill Boeing's small biplane plant on Lake Union one year earlier; the Seattle General Strike of 1919 (the only general strike in American history); the World's Fair of 1962; and the park and transit projects that occurred with the Forward Thrust bonds of the same decade. Each of these undertakings was widely criticized, even derided. Each, in its way, fortified the growing city.

Almost from the start, the city grew at a rapid pace. The Gold Rush of 1897 brought more prospective Seattle homeowners than prospectors. A brilliant public relations offensive convinced the ever-restless American that he could not go to Alaska without first spending most of his savings in Seattle. During this period, from 1890 to 1910, Seattle grew six times over. When the last of the original pioneers died in the early twentieth century, the muddy little village on the shore of Elliott Bay was a brawny city with civic leaders ready to tear down hills and open new waterways.

The Gold Rush linked Seattle and Alaska in the public mind in a way that persists to this day. Seattle, of course, is much closer to San Francisco, 843 miles to the south, than it is to Anchorage, 2,484 miles to the north. Nonetheless, Seattle's latitude, slightly above forty-seven degrees north, makes it the most northern of major American cities, which perhaps is a contributing factor to some of the

Alaskan misconceptions. The city is even farther north than Bangor, Maine, and about equal with Saint John's, Newfoundland. What this means to everyone besides armchair students of geography is that in the early summer the late light lingers until almost ten o'clock. July and August usually average less than an inch of rainfall, and Seattle gardeners, whose numbers are legion, become much like their pampered plants, cherishing the sixteen hours of daylight, bursting with fresh energy.

The flip side is a dark December when the last light leaves around four o'clock, or a January when six inches of rain may fall in thirty days. Then, precipitation is best appreciated up on a mountain, like Rainier, site of the world record for snowfall in a single winter — 1,112 inches in 1972. Much has been made of the rain, but any Seattle school kid knows that the city's average of thirty-eight inches a year is less than all the major cities on the Eastern Seaboard. Some years, such as 1985, bring only twenty-five inches of rain. The recorded temperature extremes are easy to remember: zero for the low, and one hundred degrees for the high. For the record, it is not true that Mark Twain said, "The coldest winter I ever spent was a summer in Seattle." The city was San Francisco. On average, Seattle has 158 days a year when there is some form of measureable moisture falling from the sky. While it is true the summers are generally dry, as a rule you can count on three weekends to be wet. Joel Connelly, a local journalist who spends the warm months hiking in the Cascades, says the three sure bets for seasonal storms are the Memorial Day monsoon, the Fourth of July front, and the Labor Day low-pressure system.

Most people who live in Seattle use the weather to their advantage — on the good days playing outdoors, on the bad days making good use of their proximity to a bone-dry desert, an ocean shore, or a rain forest. They travel in other ways, reading more books per capita than residents of any other American city, attending more films than all but a handful of other towns. (In contrast, their church-going is near the bottom of the national scale.)

And like it or not, the city continues to grow. A surge of newcomers has pushed the metropolitan area's population ahead of San Diego and just behind Minneapolis. Almost a third of all the people living in the state reside in the Seattle-Tacoma urban corridor.

Population growth, touted by boosters since the days of mail-order real estate schemes and Gold Rush sloganeering, does not necessarily sit well with the average resident. Emmett Watson has had no trouble recruiting for his organization, Lesser Seattle, a somewhat tongue-in-cheek group whose members call themselves agents with a mission to keep newcomers out. They send pictures to relatives of bridges torn apart by storms and the gray city under the siege of a January downpour. A typical bumper sticker promotes "The Seattle Rain Festival — September to May."

Seattle has always cultivated a sharp sense of humor. Survivors of the Depression still remember Vic Meyers, the former nightclub owner and band leader who ran, successfully, for lieutenant governor on a platform of one-liners. Asked about daylight savings time during one of his campaigns, Meyers said he didn't believe in it. "Seattle," he explained, "should have two-four time, allegro." During the worst part of the local recession of 1970, when Boeing laid off nearly two-thirds of its work force, a now legendary billboard placed near the city limits read: "Will the last person leaving Seattle turn out the lights." In fact, most out-of-work engineers stayed and helped diversify the economy.

Of course, no telling of the city's light side would be complete without a decent mention of Ivar Haglund, the mollusk mogul. Until his death in 1985, the walrus-faced old restauranteur was known to one and all by his first name. Seattle's favorite merchant jester — and later, port commissioner — Ivar was given to two-hour work days and off-key renditions of his own songs. His favorite jingle was: "No longer the slave of ambition, I laugh at the world and its shams; and I think of my happy condition, surrounded by acres of clams."

■ *Overleaf:* A harbor that never sleeps, Elliott Bay was first plumbed by Arthur Denny in 1851.

■ *Left:* Late summer light gilds the Olympic Mountains — just a ferry ride from the city's fast lanes, viewed from the roof of the Columbia Seafirst Center. ■ *Above:* In the Pioneer Square Historical District, cobblestones and lampposts have regained their former glory. ■ *Overleaf:* With its high-rises to the heavens and waterways to the world, Seattle is a major world-trade center.

■ *Above:* This artistic rendering of the killer whale, a misnamed mammal, embellishes a waterfront wall at the Edgewater Inn. ■ *Right:* Victor Steinbrueck called the Seattle Tower "the handsomest high-rise" in the city. The skyscraper is in the National Register of Historic Places.

■ *Left:* Sailing is a year-round sport in Seattle, but a winter fog, like this cloak at Leschi Marina, can chill the best of ambitions. ■ *Above:* Sun-drenched Seattle with Elliott Bay and Mount Rainier are reminders of the saying: If you can see the mountain, it is about to rain; if you can't, it *is* raining.

■ *Above:* The Pacific Northwest Ballet's annual staging of *The Nutcracker* is a Christmas tradition.
■ *Right:* Nature's artwork, a rare Seattle snow-storm, redesigns the landscape at Occidental Park.
■ *Overleaf:* An aerial view of the Port of Seattle, the source of nearly one in eight jobs in King County.

A CITY OF NEIGHBORHOODS

The snob has a difficult time being exclusive in Seattle. Ask a native where the "good" part of town is and you may end up south, in a brick Tudor along the shores of Lake Washington; or north, in a wooded glen with windows facing Mount Baker and beyond; or west, staring at a sunset in a home that hugs a Magnolia cliff; or east, in lovely Laurelhurst. Eventually, the native trying to answer such an impossible question ends up like the Oz scarecrow, arms tangled as he points in all directions.

In a city of neighborhoods, each section has charm, each has a history, each has a deli, or swimming hole, or private picnic spot where the passing of seasons is judged by the complexion of an old maple tree. In some cases, a neighborhood may have its own sounds — languages from distant lands twined with the native dialect. So, it is not unusual to hear English spoken alongside Norwegian and Swedish in Ballard; Chinese and Japanese in the International District; Italian in parts of the Rainier Valley; Filipino on Beacon Hill; and Vietnamese in Columbia City.

There are no generic neighborhoods in the city, no overnight subdivisions thrown up to match a blueprint for Anytown, U.S.A. Seattle's terrain — a glacier-gouged mix of clay and water spread around twelve hills — has long frustrated the factory approach to homebuilding. A houseboat on

Portage Bay is as much a Seattle trademark as is a Beacon Hill brick.

Originally, Seattle was built on seven hills: Beacon, First, Queen Anne, Denny, Capitol, Renton, and Profanity, so named because of the language most often heard from those trying to reach the top by Yesler Way. However, just as historians disagree over the original seven hills of Rome, some local chroniclers substitute West Seattle for Profanity. The names Renton and Profanity are seldom used now.

At least one of the original hills and parts of others are gone for good, sluiced into Elliott Bay and the Duwamish tide flats. Turn-of-the-century engineers, brought up on the man-over-matter beliefs of the Industrial Age, convinced the citizenry that Seattle could never adequately expand unless it flattened out some of those nasty slopes. They lopped off the top of two central city knolls and relieved Denny Hill of five million cubic yards, leaving the area just north of downtown with a midwestern crew cut and blunt new name — the Regrade. It is remarkable when you consider that building the Kingdome required about fifty-three thousand cubic yards of concrete — just one percent of the amount of earth taken from Denny Hill. Today, high-rise condominiums have regained some views and attracted new residents to mix with the traditional Bohemians making the Regrade a lively inner-city neighborhood.

Untouched by the earth movers and just north of the Regrade is Queen Anne Hill, at 450 feet the highest of the originals. Every year, a local Mount Everest veteran leads a charity ascent of the Counterbalance, the steep southern approach to Queen Anne. While the climb is done in good humor, the Hill is no joke: a snowstorm can mean cabin fever for its residents or provide them with an irrefutable excuse to miss work.

Some of the oldest houses in Seattle are clustered on Queen Anne, home to early-century mansions and burgundy brick chalets. Smaller, post World War II bungalows dot the center of the Hill. On the whole, they appear well-lived-in, as much a part of the scenery as the madronas which lean out toward the Sound and the overgrown ferns which thrive in the shadows. The east side of Queen Anne offers a view of the blue spine of the Cascades, while the west opens up to Elliott Bay at work and the ice-glazed Olympics. Best of all, if such views can be rated, is the full city below: a forest of office towers with the Space Needle in front and a distant Mount Rainier looming behind. Invariably, artists and visiting network news crews find themselves sharing this view, trying with paint and video to duplicate an indigenous delight.

Below, on the northwest side, lies a world of fishermen and tidy homes inhabited by families who have lived next to each other for generations. The smell of a maritime harvest near Fisherman's Terminal is enough to say, "Entering Ballard." Here, Norwegian Independence Day is a true holiday, and a visit by the King of Sweden draws thousands of loyal subjects. Hyperbole? The city's Nordic Heritage Museum cites this figure: ten thousand native-born Norwegians, eight thousand native-born Swedes, and two thousand native-born Danes live in the Seattle metro area. Attracted to the rich waters of Puget Sound and the protected finger of Salmon Bay, Scandinavians made Ballard their own town until it was annexed by the city in 1907. Lutefisk is the food of choice here, a taste that few outside Ballard have yet acquired.

Two sides of this neighborhood's personality are visible along the water. Shilshole Bay, on the west, offers calm-water berthing for an armada of sailboats and pleasure craft. Here, the sailors are of the weekend variety, well-tanned in summer. The talk is of dreamy evenings among the San Juans and second mortgages taken to keep those dreams alive. Around the corner, near the Chittenden Locks, is the home base of the nation's largest salmon and halibut fleet, where gill-netters and trollers, seiners and tenders coast in with tales of high-seas treachery. Like farmers, real fishermen never rest. The talk is of cold Alaskan waters, torn nets, and first mortgages in deep trouble. The weather, a falling market, a political decision — anything can kill a season. But when the harvest is good, life is sweet, if seasonal.

Upstream from the locks, near a blue and orange bridge (hard to miss, even in thick fog), is Fremont, an old mill town that now hosts a legendary street fair and an honorary mayor. Both are lively. Fremont is like the old friend who decided to travel for six years instead of settling into a steady job: a little scruffy, always unpredictable, but never dull. The big time arrived in 1986 when a Hollywood production team opened the first movie studio in the Northwest inside a converted warehouse complex next to the ship canal. Two Los Angeles veterans who said they were tired of life in the smog lane settled on Fremont as just this side of paradise.

Fremont shares a Lake Union shoreline and spiritual kinship with Wallingford and the lower part of the University District. Perennial students, yuppies who hate yuppies, octogenarians who cultivate year-round gardens, and everyone in between can be found here. The sturdy, middle-aged homes are often full of flourishes designed to slow the aging process. David Denny, younger brother of Arthur, built a trolley car to this destination at the turn of the century and named the area Brooklyn. The venture ruined him financially—the name did not catch on either — but the U-District prospered with the Alaskan-Yukon-Pacific Exposition of 1909. Almost an urban dream, this neighborhood has three lakes no more than a fifteen-minute stroll from any home. Cultures blend instead of clash.

Not so long ago, the city limits extended only as far northeast as Sixty-fifth Street. Following World War II, new homes sprouted like spring alder in the neighborhoods of Windermere, View Ridge, and Lake City. The newly populous districts joined older north Seattle areas such as Sandpoint and Laurelhurst. What they had in common, from the more expensive split-levels to the simpler ranch houses, was an unpretentious style. The nation's first modern shopping mall, built at Northgate in 1950, followed this migration.

Closer to the center of town, one of the city's original neighborhoods was also evolving with the post-war boom. Capitol Hill, optimistically named in anticipation of a statehouse that went to Olympia instead, acquired a more heterogenous appearance from mid-century on. Crowned by Volunteer Park, the Hill was long considered millionaire's country, and the stately homes around the

Park still bear witness to a time when top hats were the rage on Broadway. Capitol Hill is the hub of the Central District, a nucleus for doctors and nurses working the nearby hospitals and for artists painting their way through poverty. Broadway, the main street, is a river of excitement, always fast-moving. Ice-cream shops and bookstores share the street with the flamboyant and the scholarly; bronze dance steps, embedded into the sidewalk with arrows, show pedestrians how to waltz.

South of Capitol Hill, below Yesler Terrace, are the family markets and ornamented hotels of the International District, known as the second-largest Chinatown on the West Coast. Asians have always had strong ties to Seattle, based on a mostly triumphant struggle to overcome bigotry. The first Chinese settlers arrived in 1860, less than a decade after the Denny party. They worked as cheap labor until the market collapsed and riots broke out. In 1886, an angry mob tried to force Chinese immigrants at gunpoint to board a ship to the Orient. Those who chose to stay felt psychological scars lasting decades. The Japanese also had a rough time, particularly during the forced internment of World War II. Today, both cultures are an integral part of the city's good health and make strong contributions to the arts, politics, and commerce. Ethnic traditions flourish, from the reenactment of the ancient Bon Odori Festival every July to the culinary delights offered by many quality restaurants and the rich tales spun by old storytellers living in the residential hotels.

Below Capitol Hill, on the east side, are the neighborhoods of Madison Park, Madrona, and Leschi; to the south lie Mount Baker, Lakewood, and Seward Park. Rich and poor, what their residents have in common is Lake Washington. Some live on its shores; most live with a kitchen view of it. The trolley cars used to carry Sunday celebrants to a zoo and casino at Leschi and a ferry dock and bathing beach at Madison Park. The beaches fell into a period of uncertainty during mid-century, only to be revived by the miracle cleanup of Lake Washington in the early 1960s. Gentrification followed, racing up the hillsides. What nature had blessed, the lumber and hardware store enhanced.

Sailors park their boats at Leschi, Lakewood, or Madison Park. Joggers and bikers use the ideal lake trail in any weather, competing with the take-no-guff Canada geese for turf during the winter. A sunrise, bleeding orange over the Cascades, is another shared pleasure among residents in this part of the city. The old saying, "Red sky at morning, sailor take warning," may caution a fisherman in Ballard, but here it is a siren call for windsurfers or kayakers.

Between Lake Washington and Puget Sound, south of downtown, are Rainier Valley, Columbia City, Beacon Hill, the industrial area along the Duwamish, Georgetown, and West Seattle, where the city was born in a cluster of damp cabins on Alki Beach. The Rainier Valley may hold the city's most diverse ethnic mix and is the answer to the inevitable trivia question: where was Major League Baseball played outdoors for one season? At Sick's Stadium, now a light-industry plant north of Franklin High School.

Columbia City, where Rainier Avenue starts to climb, was annexed by the city about the same time West Seattle and Ballard came into the fold. Full of historical buildings, Columbia City used to have port-town aspirations, as a slough from Lake Washington covered what is now Genesee Park. West Seattle, on the other hand, dreamed even higher: its first name was New York-Alki, the last word a bit of chinook jargon meaning by and by. When the schooner *Exact* landed at Alki that grim November day, members of the Denny, Boren, Terry, Low, and Bell families disembarked in tears. New York-Alki never developed as planned, but West Seattle became a fine city on a bluff, full of working-class homes and versatile parks. The highest point in the city is here, an intersection measured at 518 feet, a mere 87 feet below the top of the Space Needle. Views of spinnakers on the Sound and tinted glass skyscrapers abound. In a city of neighborhoods, there is no better place to savor them all.

■ *Overleaf:* Magnolia Bluff is ten minutes from downtown and a glance away from Puget Sound.

■ *Above:* In Ballard, Norwegian Independence Day rivals the Fourth of July. As always, Scandinavians in this close-knit neighborhood depend on the sea for sustenance and the annual parade for festive relief. Lutefisk and pampered pastries are the favored foods during the May 17 celebration.

■ *Above:* A snooze between chores is part of the rhythm at Fisherman's Terminal in Ballard, home of the nation's largest salmon and halibut fleet.
■ *Overleaf:* Hing Hay Park in the International District is small but detailed, featuring dragon and pagoda artwork based on ancient designs.

■ *Left:* A Chinese drill team performs on a summer day. Seattle's ethnic festivals are as varied as its individual neighborhoods. ■ *Above:* When the cherry trees are on seasonal display, a stroll through the University of Washington's Quad can be a sensory treat for harried students of the "U-District."

■ *Above:* Some of the glacial melt from Mount Rainier eventually ends up in Lake Washington, but the chill is long gone by August. ■ *Right:* Lake Union is a quick escape from the residential west slope of Capitol Hill, where view apartments are snuggled next to refurbished mansions.

■ *Left:* Funky First Avenue is the main artery for a downtown neighborhood of twenty thousand residents. ■ *Above:* The Mount Baker district, clinging to a hill over Lake Washington, was developed by David Denny, the younger brother of pioneer Arthur Denny. ■ *Overleaf:* Lake Union houseboats make use of every inch of available space.

■ *Above:* A sailboat under the Aurora Bridge waits to pass through the Lake Union Ship Canal. A city of bridges and boats, Seattle is spread over twelve hills and around three lakes. Puget Sound connects to inland freshwater via the Chittenden Locks.

■ *Above:* Another face of Fremont: this motorcycle is parked in the neighborhood's lively commercial district. ■ *Overleaf:* From the crest of Beacon Hill, the traditional homes of Mount Baker look as indigenous as the towering Douglas firs.

■ *Above:* One of Seattle's oldest neighborhoods, Queen Anne Hill is known for its heart-pumping inclines and breathtaking views.

■ *Above:* Every July, Bon Odori Festival dancers in the International District reenact a Japanese ritual dating back to the tenth century.

■ *Above:* Exotic food, offbeat music, and hand-crafted specialties draw several hundred thousand people to the University Street Fair.

■ *Above:* Traditional Scandinavian folk songs fill Bergen Square in Ballard, which was a separate city until annexed by Seattle in 1907.

■ *Above:* When the carnival comes to the Rainier Valley, summer squeals fill the air. The rides are constructed on the site of old Sick's Stadium, home of the long-gone Seattle Pilots.

POCKETS OF PARADISE

Those given to occasional outbursts of regional chauvinism do not like to admit it, but Seattle owes much of its reputation as a great city for public parks to New York. It is a hard truth, difficult for a native to accept, but no more difficult than the statistic the New Yorker must swallow: Manhattan gets more rainfall than Seattle. Two New York landmarks, Central Park and Coney Island, both American icons in their way, had an indirect but undeniable influence on the young Northwest city during its park-building phase. From Central Park came competition; from Coney Island, inspiration.

First the competition. When Frederick Law Olmsted completed his design for Central Park in the 1860s, he was hailed as a genius and cities east and west requested his services. His two sons, the Olmsted brothers of Brookline, Massachusetts, carried on the family tradition. Seattle hired them in 1903 to bring together the greenbelts and patches of park scattered around a scruffy town, swollen with Gold Rush prosperity. The brothers had their father's masterpiece in mind and they went a step further. They plotted wilderness parks as chaotic as the land itself, connected by a series of elegant boulevards. At a time when city engineers were preparing to tear down hills and rip canals through the lake valleys, the Olmsteds boldly determined to follow the unique contour of the land rather than

fight it. Their grand idea was to allow continuous travel from park to park through tree-lined tunnels.

The plan, in part an elaboration of an earlier vision by a city official, was adopted in stages over the next twenty years but never quite completed as envisioned. Nonetheless, the Olmsted legacy dominates the park system, including the last stand of virgin timber at Seward Park; winding, wonderful Lake Washington Boulevard; the grand south entrance to the University of Washington; Ravenna Boulevard; Woodland Park's playful design; the boulevards on Magnolia and the north side of Capitol Hill; and the Victorian amenities of Volunteer Park, as well as a thousand little touches sometimes hidden by winter or neglect.

As inspiration, Coney Island helped make the parks palatable to city taxpayers. Why pay for raw land, many of the newcomers asked, when there is so much of it? The answer, in part, came with a series of amusement centers in private parks, which became some of the city's most beloved Sunday outing sites. To lure customers, park operators introduced everything from casino gambling and caged bears at Leschi Park to floating bandstands at Madison Park and exotic rides and saltwater bathing at Alki. When the city was able to purchase the popular private parks—or in some cases had them donated by overextended operators—their value was proven. Most of Seattle's major park purchases were made between 1900 and 1910, the most explosive growth period in its history. By the end of that first decade, a quarter of a million people lived in Seattle. More than fifty years would pass before any significant new park development began again.

But in the meantime, the Ship Canal was built. A dream of the pioneers, this enormous undertaking took seven years to complete. When the Chittenden Locks and Ship Canal finally opened in 1917, uniting Puget Sound with the great inland body of freshwater, a new shoreline was born. The lake's water level dropped a full nine feet, creating beaches and strips of greenbelt. The next time you peddle along Lake Washington Boulevard and stop for a snack on a strip of grass which used to be underwater, think of the laborers who dug the ditch.

Today, the city park system comprises 233 parks covering more than five thousand acres. The one that got away—Mercer Island—was recommended for purchase in 1910 and would have doubled total park acreage. Ah, well. If parks are indeed "the breathing lungs and beating hearts of great cities," as Mayor George Hall said a hundred years ago, Seattle is an Olympic athlete.

Periodically, a national magazine will massage the civic ego with a rave of Freeway Park, an oasis of waterfalls straddling Interstate-5 in the heart of downtown, or 520-acre Discovery Park, the city's biggest and most primeval. Just as impressive are the quarter-acre miniparks, some with stunning views, or the fragile little garden parks, as delicate as a glass vase.

Seattle parks have personalities to match an individual's mood. The Washington Park Arboretum with its ideal canoe marshes, Japanese Tea Garden, and lanes of seasonal color is a perfect place to fall in love, renew an old love, or lose yourself in an impressionistic trance. By last count, there are more than five thousand different varieties of plant life in the Arboretum. Chances are, if it can live in a temperate climate, it is living well here.

Feeling blue? The brooding loner can find no better company than the weathered redwoods stooped along the nearly five miles of trail inside West Seattle's Lincoln Park. The trail follows a windswept bluff, drops to deep-shaded meadows, then opens to the seawall above Stony Beach. Here the salt air is original, untouched by the industrial scents or gastronomic diversions found along other parts of the city's waterfront. Covering 130 acres, this is one of the city's biggest parks and a good place to hide from the cosmopolis.

Those desiring different company can find refuge in the Woodland Park Zoo or the Seattle Aquarium. The Zoo has been alternately vilified and glorified ever since the city purchased the site from an eccentric Englishman for $100,000 in 1900. Like many of its inhabitants, the Zoo has never stopped evolving. After the Olmsteds added their own paths and animal playgrounds to the formal gardens left by Gus Phinney, campaigns featuring broken-hearted lions and elephants housed in leaky sheds led to continual improvements. Today the Zoo is an award-winner and frequently named one of the top five in the country.

It does not take long to understand why. The African savanna provides everything but ancient man: giraffes, zebras, hippos, springbok, and their geographic kin roam the grasslands and frolic in the waterholes. There are no roofs. No cages. City sounds are muffled. East Africa appears. The gorillas move lightly through their own mountain valley and tropical forest. At the indoor facility next to them, some primates were so happy Zoo officials had to give them birth control pills. Their home, with record in-captivity births, was beginning to resemble a maternity ward.

Intimacy under the sea is on display at the Seattle Aquarium. A visitor can go snout-to-snout with a black-tipped shark or play at the Touch-Tank, home of sea stars, featherduster worms, and sea anemones. The lasting value of the Aquarium, however, is the view it offers of a life cycle largely invisible yet crucial to the city. Most of what goes on in Puget Sound is hidden below its surface. The Aquarium, especially its Underwater Dome, drops the land-bound human in the middle of the age-old struggle between predator and prey. It is impossible to look on Elliott Bay in the same way afterwards.

Back among the bipeds on roller skates, the people parks of Green Lake, Alki, Volunteer, and Golden Gardens provide endless varieties of the human species at play. Volunteer Park offers a Gothic water tower, a lush garden conservatory, an outdoor amphitheater and has been aptly called, "The best free view in town." Olympic sunsets, with the Pacific Science Center arches glowing in the foreground, are legendary.

In the summer, Alki Beach returns to its Coney Island roots. The sun-starved are always out in force, and hot-rodders and hamburger vendors compete for the attention of those in search of the body beautiful. Market reports confirm what many a native has long known: people in Seattle buy more suntan lotion per capita than residents of any other city in the nation, and they are not far behind the country's leading purchasers of sunglasses. Perhaps the tools of the sun trade are lost between nice days. During the warm months, Golden Gardens is much the same as Alki — full of swimmers defying the old maxim that a human being can only last about twenty minutes in the numbing waters of the Sound. A dip, even on days when the mercury dances around ninety degrees, is a bracing experience, an antidote to siesta sleepiness. In the winter, a Golden Gardens stroller can feel the sting of the wind, watch the herons swoop, and imagine Seattle before the Denny party arrived.

Green Lake. Ah, Green Lake. Colored by late-summer algae, the city's favorite all-purpose park is a north Seattle jewel created by glaciers from the last Ice Age. A sawmill used to slice timber on the northeast shore. A century ago, mom and dad packed a lunch and took a long day's hike to Green Lake. If they were lucky, they might stumble upon a deer or the occasional bear still roaming the fringe of the frontier town. By 1905, Green Lake had become part of the Olmsteds' master plan and in the following years managed to survive popularity and the serious suggestion of one civic leader that it be filled with dirt and leveled into a golf course. The loop around the lake is 2.8 miles, a course some people can run in under thirteen minutes. Most do it in about twenty-three. Diversions abound any time of year: skaters, bikers, windsurfers, and joggers pushing baby strollers. Even wildlife has a special spot: an island game reserve just south of the Bathhouse Theatre.

A jogging trail and bike path connect Green Lake to Ravenna Park, just north of the University of Washington. Ravenna Park, named by an early real estate promoter for a town in Italy, used to be famous for its ancient trees, some dating back to the Middle Ages. A creek runs through a ravine in the park, and the dark, wild-forest floor is perfect for the kind of growth usually found in an Olympic Peninsula rain forest. But what one arm of nature provided, the other took away; lightning kept striking down the oldest of the trees, thwarting a plan to preserve the grove as a tourist site. City officials were worried about safety so the last of the tall trees at Ravenna Park were ordered cut down.

Up high, out of the deep shadows, Seattle's smaller parks give the public a chance to enjoy regal property for less than a pauper's price. Kerry Park is a cozy aerie set amid the old mansions of Queen Anne Hill on West Highland Drive. Kobe Terrace, with its flowering cherry trees and four-ton stone lantern from Japan, lines up the visitor for a sweeping view of the Duwamish Valley. Denny Blaine is a half-acre swimming hole bordered by million-dollar Lake Washington homes.

Faced with a dearth of available property in recent years, Seattle has reached into the creative well for ideas to keep the park system growing. By recycling neglected land, the city has transformed old dumps and weed-choked eyesores into new parks and restful urban retreats. A sprawling parking lot in Pioneer Square was lined with trees and cobblestoned, and *Voilà!* Occidental Park thrives in the heart of the historical district. Genesee Park, now a favorite spot for soccer games and hydroplane racing fans during one mad week in August, was built over a landfill. The Army base in Magnolia shed its military trappings and was born again as Discovery Park, a haven for herons, racoons, and, on one occasion, a cougar dubbed D.B.; Navy acreage at Sandpoint became Magnuson Park. Waterfront Park transformed a soggy site at Pier 59, and Myrtle Edwards did the same for an area next to railroad tracks north of the Aquarium. Both parks were made possible by Forward Thrust, which led in the 1960s to the park system's biggest expansion since the days of the Olmsted brothers.

The most imaginative of the new additions is Gasworks Park. Converted from a noxious gas plant to a nationally praised urban playground, Gasworks is now the favorite place in town to fly a kite. Or several kites. Viewed from the sundial atop the man-made mound, downtown shines across Lake Union. The park's toxic ghosts caused an environmental scare a few years back, but the industrial relic was given the okay after re-sodding and posting of signs which read: "Please do not eat the dirt."

The ultimate recycling suggestion, made years ago in jest, no doubt, is indicative of the prevailing attitude. "Like many a native," wrote historian Stewart Holbrook, "I am privately of the opinion that this entire region should be set aside as one great park."

■ *Above:* There is no better place in Seattle to set a kite aloft than atop the man-made mound in Gasworks Park, which rose from the skeleton of an industrial plant on the north shore of Lake Union.

■ *Above:* More than five thousand types of plants grow in the Washington Park Arboretum, a crowding of color at every turn. ■ *Overleaf:* The Volunteer Park Conservatory crowns Capitol Hill.

■ *Above:* More than seventy years ago, Green Lake became part of the Olmsted brothers' master park plan and was lined with deciduous trees. The park system has grown from a donation by pioneer David Denny to five thousand public acres.

■ *Above:* Gorillas romp through the Tropical Forest at Woodland Park Zoo. ■ *Overleaf:* Green Lake, the city's favorite all-purpose park, features a 2.8-mile-long joggers' path, a neighborhood swimming hole, a backyard home for windsurfers, and, in less hectic moments, a site for waterfront solace.

■ *Above:* During the summer, when the city soaks
in sixteen hours of daylight and rain seems a distant
memory, Volunteer Park responds with a fragrant
fervor. Visitors to this Capitol Hill park can see what
has been called "the best free view in town."

■ *Above:* Those who take the winding trek through the wilderness of Discovery Park are rewarded with this vista of the West Point Lighthouse. ■ *Overleaf:* Low tide at Duwamish Head in West Seattle, near the spot where the Denny party landed in 1851.

■ *Above:* Azalea Way in the Arboretum, a treasured springtime strolling lane, was used for horse racing around the turn of the century.

■ *Above:* The Arboretum's Japanese Garden requires constant pruning and patience, but the reward is a delicate landscape of outdoor artistry.

■ *Above:* On the bluff at Lincoln Park, in West Seattle, snow muffles the sounds of the city.
■ *Right:* Landbound no more, the visitor without fins is given a rare glimpse of life under Puget Sound in the Aquarium's Underwater Dome.

■ *Left:* Amid the bustle of Pioneer Square, tiny Waterfall Garden Park offers a soothing retreat.
■ *Above:* Another urban delight, canoeing near the Arboretum on Lake Washington is most popular during the first warm weeks of spring.

■ *Above:* Jogging along the Lake Washington path just after a storm is a bracing way to stay in shape. Much of the present-day shore was under water until the Ship Canal opened in 1917, lowering the water level and leaving an expanse of new beach.

THE SPORTING LIFE

There is an old saying which explains some of Seattle's most cherished values. Usually, the line is presented to some workaholic newcomer trying to figure out what makes a native tick. "In Seattle," the saying goes, "it doesn't matter so much what you do, as what you do after work."

What we do after work is ski, sail, windsurf, hike, climb, run, bike, skateboard, swim, fly, kayak, dive, shoot, hook, bash, boot, or watch any of the above in staggering numbers. By last count, almost one of every six Seattle residents was a card-carrying member of Recreational Equipment, Inc., or REI—the nation's largest consumer co-op, founded in 1938 by frustrated local mountaineers who were tired of paying premium prices for imported climbing hardware. People camp overnight—on the sidewalk—in order to save a few dollars on a sleeping bag at REI's annual spring sale. Equally fanatical, in the fall, are the Saturday afternoon residents of Husky Stadium and the very vocal partisans who fill the Kingdome on Sunday to watch Seahawk football. Basketball fans go hot and cold. For years, the Supersonics led the National Basketball Association in attendance. A few losing seasons later, attendance hit the bottom of the league. The high point, emotionally, was 1979, when a gritty Lenny Wilkens team whipped the Washington Bullets for the World Championship. The streets were thronged with horn-honkers and intimate strangers; the city went on a week-long celebratory, back-slapping bash, topped by a grand ticker tape parade down Fifth Avenue.

Seattle has been criticized, usually by a refugee from the stratified East, for being "too mellow." As one national magazine remarked: "There are lots of people around who do some curious, out-of-way little trick that enables them to work nine hours a week and get by. Then, the rest of the time...what? Nobody knows." Perhaps. In fact, the type-A personality is here, no doubt about that, but the manic energy is channelled outdoors. Example: American Dream, Seattle style — the Million Dollar Salmon Derby. Every year, ten thousand or more fin-chasers are driven to a frenzy in pursuit of a single fish, tagged and released into Puget Sound, on a promise of instant wealth for the angler who lands it. More realistic is the lure of Lake Washington sockeye. In 1970, the sockeye returned to the lake in significant numbers, instigating a revival of freshwater salmon fishing. What joy: angling for the Northwest's favorite fish in the city's own backyard. Where else can a lawyer catch a ten-pound salmon and still make it to work on time? Throw in a sunrise bounding off the pink face of Mount Rainier and you have, in the words of no less an authority than *Sports Illustrated,* "The best place in America for the urban outdoorsman."

But there is more, much more. It is not true that there are twice as many sailboats in town as tennis rackets; it just looks that way — especially on Opening Day, the first Saturday in May, when everything from kayaks to oceanic cruisers cram the Montlake Cut to celebrate the floating life. A two-week sailing trip to Vancouver Island is a standard vacation. Feel a breeze whipping up Lake Union on a Thursday afternoon in June? Take the rest of the day off. Nobody will believe your excuse, but the odds are better in Seattle that the boss will understand.

Most weekend sailors have a saving sense of humor about their passion. Their standard witticism goes something like this:

Question: What's it like to own and maintain a fancy sailboat?

Answer: Put on several sweaters, thick pants, and a rain suit, then take a cold shower. While in the shower, try to stuff a handful of hundred-dollar bills down the drain.

Ironically, the source of this recreational paradise is the very thing that so many grumble about: rain. Warm air from the Pacific brings a continual flow of moisture-laden clouds which collide with the Olympics and the Cascades. Most of the year, the immediate by-product of this collision is snow, providing skiers with a six-month season, climbers with blue glacial challenges, and everyone else with water, water everywhere. Lake Washington, fed by the Cedar River, would be a mud puddle without years of seasonal runoff. The rain also means that all the major spectator sports are played indoors, except for the University of Washington's hardy Huskies, who have been hosting contests next to Union Bay since 1920.

This love affair with the outdoors is not some recent infatuation, a trend to fit the times. No, sir. In 1900, the city published the first map of the town's own bicycle paths — twenty-five miles of trails. At the time, there were less than a hundred thousand citizens, but they owned ten thousand bikes. Today, the trails connect the city's major parks, and Metro buses are outfitted with special bike racks to accommodate the two-wheeled commuter in need of a lift. In the early part of the century, hiking was a letter sport at the University of Washington, and before that the local Indian tribes staged footraces and lacrosse games on the beaches.

Then there is hydroplane racing. Ever since a speedboat named the *Slo-mo-shun* hit 160 miles an hour on Lake Washington in 1950, Seattle has been in love with its roostertails. A noisy, ill-defined sport that plays to the ooohs of a sudsy crowd, hydroplane racing continues to draw up to half-a-million paying spectators every year for the Seafair Race in August. The reason has less to do with competition than tradition: for years, the Seafair Race was the only big league sport in town.

There was always baseball, of the Pacific Coast League variety, and for a long time no one seemed to care whether the players were major leaguers or not. Summers passed at a leisurely pace with the Rainiers playing Sick's stadium, while Mount Rainier loomed over the right-field bleachers, and local heroes like Fred Hutchinson provided many a stirring moment. Like Husky Stadium, with its superb view of the Cascades and Lake Washington, a fan could look out and dream of one sport while watching another.

Big-time sports came to Seattle on October 20, 1967, and it all began with a loss. The Sonics dropped the city's inaugural professional basketball game to the San Diego Rockets 121 to 114 before 4,473 fans. It was not an auspicious beginning, but it was a start, and Sonics fans soon carried on an old Seattle sports tradition, love of the oddball, by cheering a totally bald, charmingly inarticulate guard named Slick Watts. With the Rainiers, fans rallied around anti-hero Ray Oyler, who came to the team with a .135 batting average and never failed to disappoint. Later, the bleacher-bound found Efren Herrera, a field-goal kicker for the Seahawks who, despite his size and slowness, also ran and tossed the ball.

The Seahawks were loved nearly to death even before they booted their first kickoff in September 1976. It was long thought that pro football and the Huskies could not coexist. Even as the concrete dome rose on the old tide flats, pessimists continued to fear one of the two big football teams would end up broke or forgotten. But by the time the Kingdome opened for business, those fears were gone. The Seahawks had produced one of the largest advance season ticket sales in the history of the sport — 57,000 tickets gone, for every game. At the same time, Coach Don James was building a national powerhouse out of the Huskies.

The Mariners opened for business in the Kingdome in 1977, bringing Major League Baseball back to town after a single year in old Sick's Stadium in 1969. But the Dome is not just a spectators' arena. The Emerald City Marathon brings runners stumbling in, after an unforgettable survey of Seattle. Like the popular Seafair ten-kilometer run through downtown, the marathon is a fine fusion of sport and city — two things which have gone together since the pioneers concluded there was more to do in the rain than moan.

■ *Above:* The long waiting list for a space at the Shilshole Bay Marina adds weight to that oft-heard claim that Seattle is the boating capital of the world.
■ *Overleaf:* Troubles fade away as fast as the spinnakers fill on a summer eve at Shilshole.

■ *Above:* Major League Baseball, after one season outdoors in 1969, returned to Seattle when the Kingdome opened. A Mariner fan can get peanuts, popcorn, and an instant replay on the television set overhead — creature comforts of indoor ball.

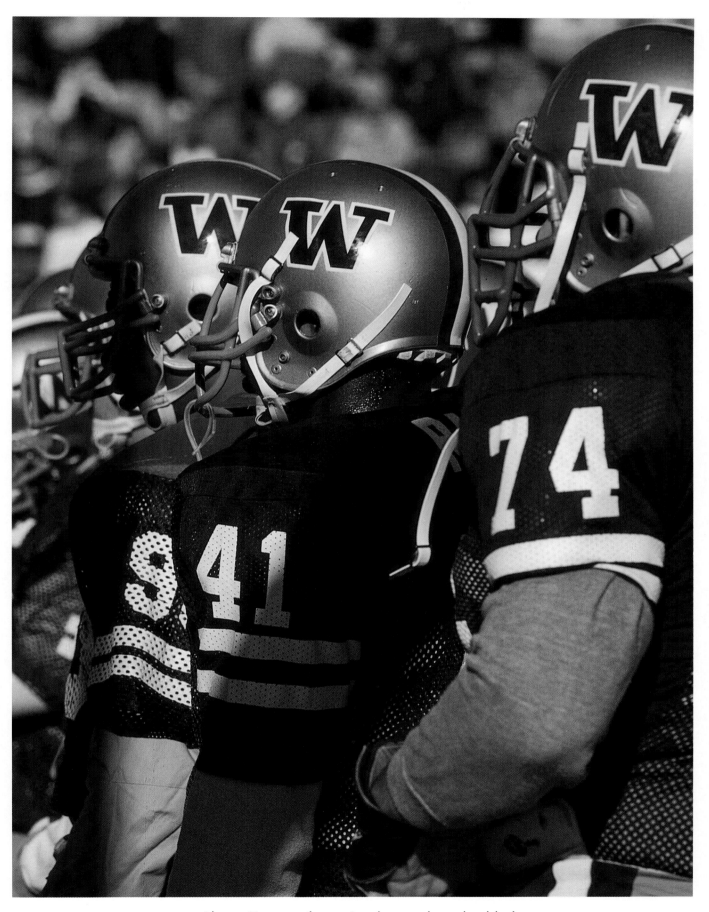

■ *Above:* Towers of tenacity, the purple and gold of the University of Washington are the colors of a national football powerhouse. ■ *Overleaf:* Another sold-out game on a sun-kissed day in Husky Stadium, the home of "the dawgs" since 1920.

■ *Left:* In midsummer, a game of pickup volleyball at Alki Beach may get hot and heavy. Most players forget the score by sunset. ■ *Above:* Horse racing at Longacres Racetrack is a favorite pastime for the lucky and the near-lucky.

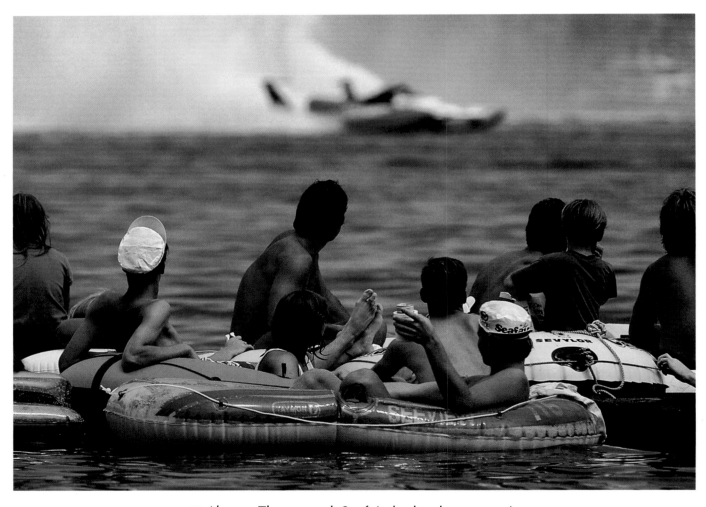

■ *Above:* The annual Seafair hydroplane race is supposed to be a spectator sport, but fans tend to become part of the act as the mercury climbs.
■ *Right:* During the salmon season, there is always room in Elliott Bay for another urban angler looking for a day's worth of bragging rights.

■ *Left:* A ten-kilometer footrace is staged before the Opening Day Regatta in the Montlake Cut.
■ *Above:* Fans come from as far away as Anchorage, Alaska, to scream for the National Football League Seahawks. ■ *Overleaf:* If the fish beneath this Elliott Bay pier are not biting, a view of the Olympic Mountains provides consolation.

■ *Above:* A Seattle Pacific University crew slices
through the water at the Montlake Cut. Boosted by
a Seattle Parks Department program, team rowing
is a sport which has caught on all over the city.

■ *Above:* Prime dock space at Lake Union marinas can fetch a premium price. But few Seattle sailors complain about the location — close enough to downtown that chasing a balmy breeze is just minutes away from the central city office core.

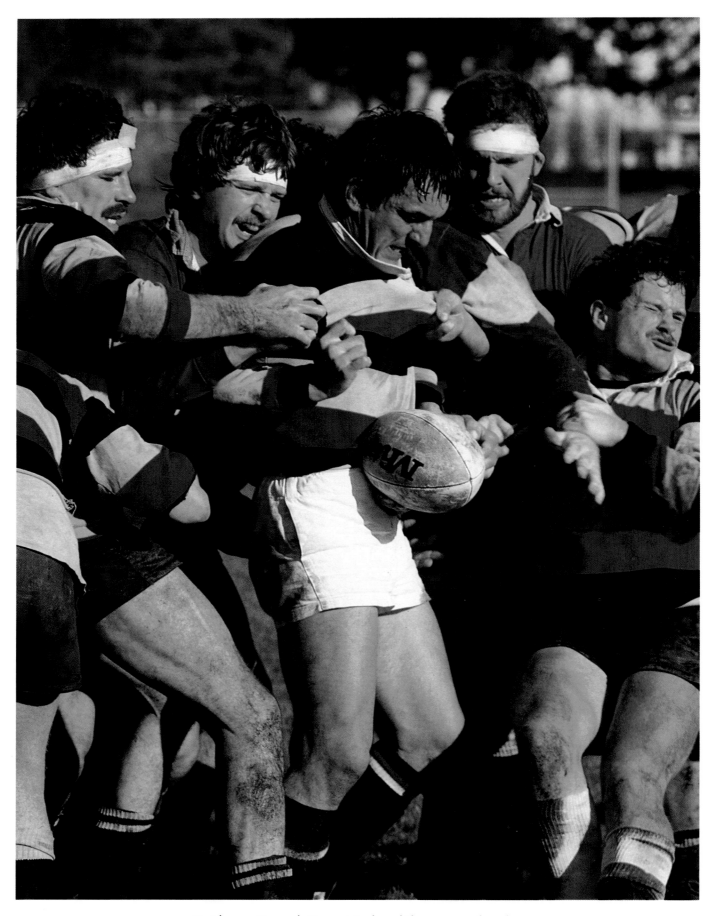

■ *Above:* Crunch time. Mud and the game of rugby were made for each other, and lower Woodland Park is a good place to watch the two come together in regular, hard-hitting contests.

A CITY TO MATCH THE SETTING

City builders trying to construct something of lasting value and beauty in Seattle have always run into one formidable wall of competition: Mother Nature. As Murray Morgan noted, "The scenery is better than if it had been planned." It may not be difficult to improve upon barren grasslands in Kansas, with nary a knoll to break the plain, or Oklahoma scrublands, flat-baked under the southwestern sun, but how does anyone match a site featuring the bluffs of Magnolia with the Olympics framed between red-barked madronas?

Initially, the pioneers shrugged and whacked away at what they could. They built everything with wood; it was, for a long time, all they had. Neat plats of wood-frame houses and the occasional two-story general store rose in accordance with a model based in part on Cleveland and in part on Cherry Grove, Illinois. The experiment with midwestern symmetry and indigenous building materials ended dramatically on June 6, 1889, after a cabinetmaker spilled boiling glue on a basement floor and the town went up in flames. The inferno raced up the hillsides, swallowing wood-planked sidewalks and homes. The Great Fire burned twenty-five blocks clean to the ground. A total of fifty-eight blocks in one hundred twenty acres was ruined. Photographs taken the day after show a smoldering heap, much like towns decimated by World War II fire-bombing. In retrospect, many architectural historians believe the fire was the best thing to happen to Seattle.

Almost immediately, a new city rose from the ashes, one built of stone and masonry and ornamented with loving touches of terra-cotta. The best evidence of this is one of Seattle's oldest structures —the six-story Pioneer Building at First and Yesler, built the same year as the fire. With its stone-arched entranceway and rock-support systems, the Pioneer Building greeted Gold Rush prospectors with the same face it offers tourists and lawyers who people the Square today.

Another Pioneer Square institution is the Maynard Building on First Avenue, one of the few landmarks named for the man some historians call the true father of Seattle — Doc Maynard. A quirky medical doctor who often preferred the company of Indians to his fellow midwestern transplants, Maynard also brought commerce and far-sighted vision to the young city. He was long dead when the Maynard Building rose on the site of Seattle's first bank — a den of coffee barrels stashed full of money, which was managed by Dexter Horton.

A good capsule view of the city's architectural history can be obtained by taking a few steps back from the Pioneer Building and looking up Yesler or First Avenue to the northeast, toward the center of downtown. Both are stunning glimpses, full of clashing styles that have melded over the years. One sees the low-rise brick and stone buildings constructed just after the fire, taller turn-of-the-century beauties with a few 1920s Art-Deco styles sprinkled among them; mid-century glass and steel skyscrapers, and finally the tall new additions — dramatic, neo-classical buildings, flat-topped, arched, and peaked. There are some blights, some bland boxes, and some truly inspirational creations. The best epitomize local architect James Olson's maxim that a building becomes an art form when it works with nature.

The Arctic Building on Third Avenue and the Hoge Building on Second are full of strong colors and lively terra-cotta details, including walrus heads. But the early century's crowning achievement is the Smith Tower, built in 1914 and still a popular favorite. Named for L. C. Smith, who made his fortune in pistols and typewriters, and elegantly embellished with old-style craftwork, the Smith Tower is forty-two stories of glory with real humans inside operating the last of the city's non-automatic elevators. During the last few years of his life, Ivar Haglund owned the Smith Tower. True to character, he hung an enormous kite in the shape of a fish from its 500-foot apex. City bureaucrats tried to make him take it down, but they were besieged with angry phone calls. The kite stayed.

Much of the early twentieth century was spent tearing away at the natural environment. It was the era of massive regrade projects, the Ship Canal, Duwamish dredging, and overnight commercial building. But a light from Paris landed in Seattle in 1908 in the form of Carl Gould. A New York native, Gould had studied architecture in France and arrived in Seattle full of ideas from the Academy of the Beaux-Arts, which emphasized classical European styles. He and the times were made for each other. The city, teeming with visitors to the Alaskan-Yukon-Pacific Exposition of 1909, was trying to become a world-class center. The University of Washington, site of the Exposition, was trying to expand. Gould answered both longings. For the University he designed Suzzallo Library, a great Gothic structure that practically forces meditation on the restless student, and he contributed to the school's Quad, a tree-lined avenue reminiscent of old Europe. Off campus, Gould designed the Olympic Hotel, which opened in 1924 to raves and he won international acclaim for the Seattle Art Museum, the modified Art-Deco masterpiece.

If set to music, Art-Deco would be jazz. The loudest local versions include the very unbashful Woolworth Building and the Seattle Tower, once called "the handsomest high-rise in Seattle."

The forties, fifties, and early sixties were relatively quiet times for downtown architecture. Then two boom periods occurred, one in the sixties, one in the eighties. In the sixties the skyline moved upward and outward, became glossier and denser. Seattle was a city constantly in labor pains. The first big arrival—called the box the Space Needle came in—was the fifty-story Seafirst Building. Friends of the Smith Tower mark the date, 1964, as the year the Tower lost its premier height status for good. Seafirst was followed by the Bank of California Building, a soaring replica of Rockefeller Center and Mayor Charles Royer's favorite skyscraper. The late Minoru Yamasaki, a 1934 University of Washington graduate who went on to world fame, added the Rainier Bank Tower.

The First-Interstate Building, forty-eight stories of angled beige, helped break the reign of the box, and Fred Bassetti brought the high-rise to the pedestrian with his unique stairway design around the Federal Office Building. Bassetti was worried that tall buildings would make the average person feel threatened, so he designed terraced benches on the Federal Building's south side. Nothing makes him happier, he says, than to see the noon-time sun-seekers positioned around the steps.

All the new cloud-busters were surpassed by Martin Selig's Columbia Seafirst Center. Almost a thousand feet of dark glass, curved and graduated in seventy-six stories, the Center was the tallest building on the West Coast when it was completed in 1984. Selig, who came to Seattle as a boy fleeing Hitler's Germany and went on to own a third of all the city's office space, started an instant controversy with his instant landmark. Some derided it. Some applauded it. No one could ignore it.

For better or worse, Selig challenged Seattle. In response to his dark tower, a flurry of skyscrapers clad in creamy white or mauve was proposed for the late eighties and early nineties.

On a smaller level, First Avenue went from a mecca of pornography and Navy surplus stores to imaginative condominium complexes and impressive new hotels. While some lamented the loss of a colorful low-life district with historic roots, others saw an important new wave. And with the transformation, Art-Deco came full circle: Cornerstone completed the twenty-two-story Watermark Tower, a building with Jazz Age zest. From a ferry on Elliott Bay, the Tower is a perfect foreground contrast to the black and beige citadels of commerce rising behind it. Bathed in late light, the whole setting is a small human complement to the natural treasures left by the last Ice Age.

■ *Above:* Once the tallest structure in the city, the 605-foot-tall Space Needle is now dwarfed by a cloud-scraping skyline. ■ *Overleaf:* The compliments are still coming in for Carl Gould's modified Art-Deco masterpiece, the Seattle Art Museum at Volunteer Park — home of the world's most extensive collection of Mark Tobey paintings.

■ *Above:* The Evergreen Point Floating Bridge, connecting Bellevue to Seattle, is the longest floating span in the world. ■ *Right:* Design styles change, but beauty stays in fashion. The pyramidal tops of the King Street Station and the cherished Smith Tower rise against the beige First Interstate Center and the boxy Seafirst Bank Building.

■ *Left:* Even a whisper carries well inside the Renaissance-styled Saint James Cathedral, which was built in 1912 and is the mother church of Seattle's Catholic Diocese. ■ *Above:* For a few years, the Kingdome roof was concrete gray. White paint brought out the clean structural lines and matched the Olympic Mountains' year-round snow.

■ *Above:* The arch of the Aurora Bridge, 135 feet above Lake Union, frames the city. ■ *Right:* The twin domes of Saint James Cathedral compete for cloud space with the seventy-six-story Columbia Center —Seattle's tallest building. ■ *Overleaf:* A Carl Gould masterpiece, Suzzallo Library rises in the heart of the University of Washington campus.

■ *Left:* Suzzallo Library's Graduate Reading Room evokes a Gothic cathedral. ■ *Above:* Terra-cotta ornamentation, such as this Cobb Building Indian head, has been restored on many downtown buildings. ■ *Overleaf:* The Washington State Convention Center, with 371,000 square feet, was built in a parklike setting over I-5 in the heart of the city.

■ *Above:* Between Elliott Bay and the new sky-scrapers, parts of old Seattle have been paved over, rebuilt, and restored. Seattle's commercial core has withstood the Great Fire of 1889, two structure-rattling earthquakes, and major regrade projects.

■ *Above:* First United Methodist Church, built in 1907, is a domed diversion amid the high-rises of Fifth Avenue. ■ *Overleaf:* Terra-cotta walrus heads on the Arctic Club Building glower in their original, full-tusked ferocity. ■ *Following page:* The south entrance of Watermark Tower displays some of the detail of a new building with old esthetic values.

THE MAGIC MARKET

What makes a city? Monuments of glass and steel? A tennis court in every neighborhood? A place to work, a place to play, and a place to park? In varying degrees, yes, they all matter. But what really separates a collection of houses and businesses bound by a string of stoplights from a great city are the diverse, daily surprises. At Seattle's Pike Place Market, a grab bag of global amenities is gathered in one corner of garrulous chaos.

The Market, ever moving, ever changing, never passive, never bored, is a good nominee as the city centerpiece. As Roger Sale wrote in *Seattle, Past to Present:* "For many people the Market is Seattle, its one great achievement, the place they love most, the place they take visitors first." Consumer tastes come and go, but the Market's appeal has never diminished. Even as the shadows of futuristic office towers creep over the rickety fish stalls, even as salmon-colored condos cling to old hobo haunts, the Market pulses.

Cross First Avenue at Pike Street and there you are: capitalism in its most raw and rowdy form, with a human face. Buy a newspaper from Bangkok at the corner newstand; turn around and order a slice of spiced pizza from one of the city's oldest Italian delis; move farther down past jo-jos baking behind red lights, where fish vendors assault you with their unbeatable prices and infectious banter.

Laugh at the geoducks, or, better yet, send one to your cousin in Bloomington. Poke the crabs. Eye the octopi. But don't fondle the sea urchins.

Turn the corner, the produce is on display—stalls of bright-scrubbed carrots and exotic roots with apples here, peaches there, and an occasional imported kumquat. Move along. Bonsai growers are waiting patiently, patiently, for the stroller in the mood to buy a midget shrub. Here are shades of jade, jewelry stalls, homespun wool, rainbow kites. More relaxed than the fresh food vendors, these merchants know their handiwork will be just as valuable tomorrow. So sit and chat.

Look out toward the water. The Olympics may shape a silhouette against the moody sky. Cross the cobblestoned street. A scent of old Morocco drifts by. Sip a cup of cafe au lait, before or after the Vietnamese catfish soup. Musical ambience is nearby, in the form of an Elvis Presley impersonator crooning an a cappella version of "You Ain't Nothing But a Hound Dog." Throw him a few quarters, but save some change for the string quartet playing a melody a few international flavors away from the blind folk guitarist.

All of this has been going on, in one form or another, since 1907, when a small group of truck farmers opened a few produce stands as a way to cut out the middleman. Many were Japanese — Issei settlers who farmed the Duwamish Valley and provided, at one time, up to 75 percent of the produce for the city.

Artist Mark Tobey found his best inspiration in the Market's ebb and flow. For days on end during the Depression he came and studied faces and listened to the rhythms of commerce, the hectoring voices of crab merchants and halibut hawkers. "It needs no help," said Tobey of the Market. "It passes fast enough. People not pressed for time will find their own patterns of intricate beauty."

The Market did need help once, in 1971, when it took a citizens' initiative to ensure preservation. The leader of the campaign was Victor Steinbrueck. When he died in 1985, they named the little park with the totem pole just north of the Market after him. Now a well-used spot, it is a museum of human diversity, like the Market itself.

■ *Above:* No middleman here. Pike Place Market produce stalls offer fresh-scrubbed fruit and vegetables direct from nearby truck farms.

■ *Above:* The annual Market Street Fair is much like the Pike Place Market itself: unpredictable, fast-moving, widely entertaining, and a terrific bargain.

■ *Above:* Commerce with a human face, part of the charm of the Market is found in the interchange between buyer and seller. Computerized prices are not found in this charming corner of Seattle.

■ *Above:* A Seattle landmark, the Market sign and clock is a favorite terminus when the New Year's Eve countdown begins. ■ *Overleaf:* Dungeness crabs, plucked from the nearby waters of icy Puget Sound, beckon buyers with claws of tender meat.

■ *Above:* Artisans and craftspeople need a bit more patience than the fresh-food vendors. The Market, which opened to large crowds in 1907, has been part of a protected historical district since 1971.

THE CENTER OF ATTENTION

They started pouring concrete into a triangular pit at the foot of Queen Anne Hill one day in May 1961. The neighborhood was nothing special: a few shabby storefronts, some homes in need of paint, a couple of sailor bars with 6 A.M. happy hours. By the time they were done, the longest continuous cement pour in history had swooshed by — 467 truckloads in all — and Seattle had an instant landmark. Thus was born the Space Needle, a star that graced the cover of *Life Magazine* twice in one year.

Slender, graceful, unique, the Needle was a hit beyond the wildest dreams of the group of scrappy Seattle planners trying to organize a world's fair around a vague scientific theme. Observers say Eddie Carlson, president of the fair commission, broke down in tears as the concrete gushed into place. After all, it was Eddie who first sketched a rough outline of the Space Needle on a cocktail napkin. Victor Steinbrueck was brought in for design work, adding class and tradition to the shoe-string Needle budget of $4.5 million. Suddenly, after all the doubts, it looked as if they might pull off the World's Fair. And they did, in grand style. The Century 21 Exposition drew almost ten million visitors between April and October 1962.

John Glenn, a man of the right stuff, came and talked about the space exhibits, as did his colleague in frontier exploration, Russian cosmonaut Gherman Titov. Richard Nixon posed in front of the Needle. Robert Kennedy tried to keep track of his ever-expanding brood. Royalty was well represented, from the ill-fated Shah of Iran to England's Prince Phillip, who endeared himself with a quote about the joys of rain: "Let cats and lizards rejoice in basking in ever-lasting sunshine ... mists and drizzles and even occasional light rains make sunshine all the more welcome and constitute the proper environment of man."

That most American form of royalty, the celebrity, also showed up. Elvis Presley, just out of the Army and trying to live up to his name as the King of Rock and Roll, used the fairgrounds as a backdrop for one of his most forgettable films, *Meet Me At the World's Fair*. Later, when the Fair was all over, Warren Beatty poked in and around the Needle as the star of the psychological thriller, *The Parallax View*. The Needle, as they say in show business, had legs — true staying power.

Now the main draw of the seventy-four-acre Seattle Center, the Needle may be lit up in a brilliant UFO display, it may host a giant inflatable crab, dubbed "Louie" by the locals, or it may serve as the favorite sunset dinner site for out-of-town guests. Just as the Alaskan-Yukon-Pacific Exposition of 1909 led to an explosion of culture and growth at the University of Washington, the 1962 Fair hot-wired Seattle in ways that are still being felt.

After the Fair, successful campaigns championed new parks, road and transportation improvements, clean water and, the big plum for sports fans — the Kingdome. Before long, Seattle had a trio of prominent professional sports teams and several new cultural diamonds. All because of the Fair? No. But the glittery new exhibits of 1962 showed Seattle the way.

In retrospect, many of the science displays and predictions — floating cars, a glass dome covering downtown — may seem a little silly, and most of the permanent structures still look, well ... futuristic. But the Monorail, an elevated train which whisks passengers from the Center to downtown in ninety seconds; the Needle; and the white Gothic arches in front of the Pacific Science Center have become Seattle symbols.

Most world fairs close down before the creditors catch up with the operators. Seattle's fair made a small profit, a distinction that is still the envy of urban dreamers around the world. But it is a minor crime to define the Fair's success in bottom-line terms. Its legacy is not only a city cultural center, used year-round by sports fans and opera buffs, but a tourist mecca that is Seattle's number one visitor attraction. The Pacific Science Center, for example, is never without company, even on the dreariest winter day. Some come just to stare at the arches and throw pennies in the fountain, both Minoru Yamasaki creations. He drew the 110-story twin towers of New York's World Trade Center, but few in Seattle would trade King Kong's one-time hangout for the pleasing touches of the Center's arches. A scientific playhouse awaits the visitor inside five buildings, each full of exhibits designed to be what are called "hands-on" experiences. One can step inside the miniature mouth of a volcano, start a small mudflow, be dazzled by optical illusions, defy gravity, or walk among life-sized dinosaurs. The laser light show at the Spacearium Theater is the astral equivalent of the Aquarium's spectacular underwater performances.

Another permanent structure, the Coliseum, helped bring major league sports to Seattle. The Sonics began their playing days there, moved on to a mostly unhappy residency at the Kingdome, then came back home. Because of its unique design — the roof bends and flexes in nasty weather — the Coliseum contributed a footnote to sports history when a small leak during one Sonic game in 1986 caused the only pro-basketball rain-out. The Beatles and Bruce Springsteen have played the Coliseum, as have science fiction buffs, home computer shows, the Rolling Stones, and the kings and queens of country, soul, and gospel music.

A becalming antidote to a rock show is the International Fountain. Designed in the shape of a sunflower, the fountain's 217 nozzles are rigged to a computer program, and the result is a flow of classical music and water. People who began a tour of the Seattle Center with ambitious plans have seen their day dribble away in hours of soothing diversion. Kids love to play near the sprays and a favorite trick is to figure out the timing of the nozzles and dodge the bursts of water. Parents do not always appreciate the hijinks.

But then, kids do not always understand the elegant dance steps of the stylish partners on display next door at Center House. One day, music from the Jazz Age whirls couples around the wooden floor. Another day, the Big Band Era is played out, and oh, how the wartime romance stories start to flow with the toot of the trumpet. For many, a night of dancing on the floor at the Center House is a tumble back in time.

The question, "What are we doing this weekend?" was not always easy to answer before the cultural growth that came to the Center after the Fair. Now the question is, "How do we fit it all in?" The Opera House is home to the Pacific Northwest Ballet Company, the Seattle Symphony, and the Seattle Opera, including the widely hailed cycles of Wagner's *Ring*. A stunning addition, the Bagley Wright Theatre joined the Opera House in 1983. Praised for its sleek design and named for one of the city's driving artistic boosters, the modern stage is home to the Seattle Repertory Theatre, known as The Rep, which presents six plays a season.

Culture on a more populist level sweeps in with the annual arrival of several major festivals. The best-attended is the four-day Labor Day fest, Bumbershoot, named for the British word for umbrella, a tool which most Seattle residents prefer to ignore. Sponsored by the city, Bumbershoot is food of the world, dancing in the grass, wacky go-cart races, and lofty musical arrangements, along with craftspeople who emerge from months of unseen labor with their artwork in full blossom and a story to go with each sale. The celebration carries on an ancient tradition, for the Center was once the site of Indian potlatch festivals. Here, centuries ago, tribal chiefs held gift-giving exchanges. Now, if you look with the mind's eye and listen, you can feel the resonance of the years on the landscaped grounds.

■ *Right:* The Space Needle, Seattle's most famous landmark, is framed by the *Olympic Iliad*.

■ *Left:* A ride in the Fun Forest is a cure for feet flattened out by a long tour of the Seattle Center. ■ *Above:* Face-to-face with a mime is one way to get personally involved in the popular Folklife Festival on the Center's grounds. ■ *Overleaf:* Minoru Yamasaki's famed Pacific Science Center arches match the mood of a winter sky.

■ *Above:* Seattle Center visitors will use any excuse to dance, and this marimba band makes it easy to move and sway. ■ *Right:* The Pacific Science Center is one of the permanent — and most popular — legacies of the 1962 World's Fair.

■ *Left:* A child plays a game trying to cap one of the 217 nozzles on Seattle Center's International Fountain. ■ *Above:* Some people believe the Space Needle will always look futuristic.

■ *Above:* A blues band belts out a number at the Bumbershoot Arts Festival inside the Arena.

WATERWAYS TO THE WORLD

In his time, it sounded preposterous. One day, said Doc Maynard, America would do more trade with Japan and China than with the nations of Europe. Often ignored, Doc's remarks were regarded as the well-intentioned whiskey talk of a likeable drunk. Yet Maynard, the man who put Seattle on the map as the terminus for the transcontinental railroad, was the first of many merchants in town to look even further west, coining the phrase, "Seattle—Gateway to the Orient."

In the late twentieth century, you can not go to a meeting of any business significance in Seattle, walk by the bright shops of the waterfront, or stand within hard-hat range of a container ship's cranes without hearing Doc's very words—and more. His prophecy was realized: the country does more trade with the nations of the Pacific Rim than with Europe, and a great deal of that trade goes in and out of Elliott Bay. More than a hundred years after Doc's death, the city built around the bay is a world-class exchange center not just of goods and raw materials but of ideas and culture. The image has been embraced so strongly in Seattle that some have taken to redefining the city—as the hub of the international Pacific Northeast.

The Port of Seattle is alive—with the nation's largest ferry fleet; with enormous cargo ships bringing finished goods in from Japan and sending apples, potatoes, timber, and seafood west; with chatter of the language of commerce. The figures are astonishing: fully one out of every eight jobs in King County is tied to the Port.

It was Peter Puget, a British lieutenant on board Captain Vancouver's ship *Discovery,* who gave his name to the long body of saltwater. Vancouver was looking for an inland passage. It was not until the arrival of the Denny party that the potential of a port was discussed. Arthur Denny tied a horseshoe to a clothesline and dragged it across Elliott Bay. To his surprise, the protected Bay was very deep.

As the town grew, sailing ships and steamers filled the harbor. The most significant arrival was the steamship, *Portland,* loaded down with Alaskan gold. The banner headlines which followed set off the rush for Alaska and brought even more riches and marine traffic to Seattle.

Superlatives—of size, depth and volume—have long been attached to the waterways of Seattle, home of the world's first floating bridge (from the Mount Baker area to Mercer Island) and the world's longest floating bridge (from Union Bay to Bellevue). Dreamers suggested building a bridge across the Sound, but these notions seldom rose beyond the bowl of an engineer's pipe — thanks to public affection for a ferry fleet that carries up to 20 million passengers a year. Despite complaints of price hikes and heavy traffic, the ferries are a part of the Seattle experience; native grousing is a way of showing love, and residency. It has been calculated that if all the cars using the ferry system in one year formed a single line south, a bumper-to-bumper traffic jam would stretch to the Mexican border.

These thoughts usually vanish once the boats are chugging across the Sound, trailed by seagulls, with the scent of salt air mixing with a faint smell of diesel oil. From the stern side is Doc Maynard's town, polished and packed with sea-going ships. From the bow, the Olympics rise, and beyond that, the Orient and the future—all within reach.

■ *Overleaf:* Freighters and tugs are as much a part of the cityscape as the Kingdome.

■ *Left:* Part of the nation's largest ferry fleet, a boat heads homeward between silhouettes of the Olympics and the Kingdome. ■ *Above:* Up to twenty million passengers use Washington's ferry system every year. ■ *Overleaf:* Whether it provides food for the solo fisherman or working dock space for Harbor Island, Elliott Bay is vital to Seattle.

THE WORKING LIFE

Mike Coomes is a Seattle cop, born east of the mountains, who spent one frustrating year in law school before deciding he would rather go after people with a badge than a briefcase. Before that, he toyed with the idea of becoming a priest, flirted with journalism, sold Christmas trees in a parking lot, and took enough medieval history courses to bore a monk. Now, he is happy, or at least content. He has found a place in the city he has come to love. In the fall, he puts on a football uniform and knocks heads with lawmen from Pierce County in the annual Bacon Bowl charity game played at the Kingdome. He likes that. It keeps the fantasy alive: one day the Seahawks might need a reserve defensive back ...

But what really tickles Coomes is the drive to work. Every day as he crosses the University Bridge, he looks west at the Olympics, east at the Cascades, and smiles. Even if the mountains are veiled behind sheets of angry rain, and the sun has been hiding so long it is officially missing, he smiles. He asks, "Who would ever want to live anywhere else?"

That is the refrain heard time and again from the white collars, blue collars, and new collars who make up Seattle's work force. Fast-trackers may come barging through with a five-year plan to make top management and then cash out their equity and

move on, but by year number two, maybe number three, they are repeating the old question: "Who would ever want to live anywhere else?"

It is a problem, this old refrain. It gives the jitters to those who think Seattle is big enough and helps employers on a national recruitment search. Judging by its history, Seattle is a tough place to pass through. The city is full of workers, or sons and daughters of workers, who thought they would be doing just that. Look at the Gold Rush. It was, for all practical purposes, a flash in the rusty pan, fed by rumor and wild exaggeration. Some people tapped a gold vein in the frigid Klondike of 1897. Most did not. Many of them ended up in Seattle broke—but soothed by the temperate climate and the possibilities of a young city on a roll.

The same thing happened during World War II. Just before the War broke out, the Boeing Airplane Company was a mildly successful manufacturer, employing four thousand people in its plant along the Duwamish. By the peak of the War in 1944, Boeing's payroll had expanded ten times over—to fifty thousand workers. Overnight, Seattle was overrun by skilled engineers and semi-skilled riveters cranking out the B-17 and other bombers to fight Hitler and Hirohito.

But when the War ended and Boeing began to reduce its work force, most of the newcomers stuck around. There is, and always has been, a sense that the city is small enough for one person to find a niche, buy a house, and go camping in the summer. And small enough for one person to make a difference. Seattle was long known as a labor town: home of the Industrial Workers of the World, or Wobblies, who formed out of the mass of workers drawn to Seattle for the Ship Canal and regrade projects; home of the General Strike of 1919; home of Dave Beck's powerful Teamsters; home of shipyard workers and lumbermen.

The labor image persists, but today Seattle is primarily a service town, a city of engineers and entrepreneurs, a high-tech health center, a place with a large university population. There are still plenty of fishermen. And there are longshoremen and ship builders and steelworkers busting backs as before. But the transformation between 1970 and

1990 from a resource to a service economy has been a shift of such monumental proportions that Seattle is said to have the nation's highest proportion of middle-class residents.

There were frequent bleak times, just before the strike or during the Depression, when a village of ramshackle sheds, called Hooverville, rose on grounds near the Kingdome site. Broken men combed the nearby beach for bark and haunted the railyards for bits of coal — fuel to feed a fire on damp nights. But even during the bad times, some people dreamed in technicolor.

John Nordstrom was one, an American success story with a Seattle twist. A Norwegian immigrant, Nordstrom stepped off the boat at Ellis Island with five dollars in his pocket. After working his way west through odd mining and logging jobs, he headed for the corner of the continent and scraped for gold in Alaska. He was lucky. With his Klondike stake, he set up shop in a Seattle shoe store at Fourth and Pike. Business was not great, initially, but the store developed a good reputation and he prospered, eventually turning the store over to his sons Elmer, Everett, and Lloyd. The business expanded during the post-war years and branched out into clothing. Today Nordstrom is the nation's leading specialty apparel retailer and one of the reasons Seattle is a hub for the clothing business.

The Boeing saga was different, based more on world events and government contracts. Born in Detroit and educated at Yale, Bill Boeing was operating a furniture store and lumberyard in Seattle when the flight bug bit him. He thought he could improve on some of the planes he had piloted and he set out to build his own model inside a red barn on Lake Union. Working with some of the furniture store employees, he and a partner assembled their first plane in 1916 — the B & W, a 2,800-pound biplane with pontoons. Boeing himself took the first test flight. By 1928, financed by federal contracts, Boeing's barn was a complex on the Duwamish and one of the nation's largest aircraft builders. World War II was a major expansion period—12,000 Flying Fortresses were built. It was followed by the jet age and the company's successful entries: the 707, the popular 727, the stubby 737, the jumbo-sized 747 (twenty-three yards short of a football field in length), the 757, and the 767. Plants now operate in Everett, Kent, and Renton. Employment peaked above 100,000 workers in 1967, just before a severe recession knocked out much of the company's local work force. Instead of collapsing, Seattle's economy diversified. Boeing gradually rebounded with banner years in 1984 and 1985.

What the typical Boeing worker, top management at Nordstrom, and the fisherman in Ballard may have in common is a University of Washington degree. During the school year, about fifty thousand people work or study on the site of the old 1909 World's Fair. On one side, bordering the Montlake Cut, doctors probe for a cancer cure and experiment with edge-of-the-future genetic research. On the other side, students surge in and out of classrooms in numbers unforseen by the school's first president, a restless twenty-two-year-old named Asa Mercer. Seattle chose a college instead of a penitentiary and used its territorial grant to construct a wood-frame university building on a downtown hill in 1861. The problem was that the school had no students, which gave Mercer a lot of free time. On his own, he collected funds from the love-starved single men of the settlement and went east in search of women. He returned with eleven potential brides. This novel enterprise did little for the University, except to bring the school's first president worldwide publicity charging he was a white-slaver from a barbaric burgh.

From these Wild West origins, Seattle became a fine college town and eventually a regional research and academic center which serves as a base for hundreds of spin-off industries. As a result, high-tech with local brains, such as Microsoft in Redmond, developed on a significant scale. The University also helped Seattle grow into a foremost medical center, with national health models such as Medic One, Children's Orthopedic Hospital, and Group Health Co-op.

But the typical worker is not thinking of ill health. He is sunning himself downtown on a bench overlooking Puget Sound, thinking, "Who would ever want to live anywhere else?"

■ *Above:* Seattle is not a "company town," but Boeing has long been the city's biggest employer. In varying stages of production, new 737s move through Boeing's Renton plant.

■ *Above:* Architect Fred Bassetti designed the steps of the downtown Federal Building as a pleasant relief for the city worker. ■ *Right:* The first light of a summer day illuminates Columbia Center, kept gleaming by window-washers.

■ *Left:* Construction jobs with high-rise views are common during the current boom in downtown office building. ■ *Above:* The shipyards on Harbor Island have played a colorful and historical role in the development of the city's labor force.

■ *Above:* A portrait of the working family and a treasured piece of outdoor art, Richard Beyer's *Waiting for the Interurban* has caused many a double take in the Fremont neighborhood.

THE FRONTIERS OF CULTURE

A visitor was planning to attend the Seattle Symphony one night in early spring, not sure what to expect. She dressed in elegant evening style, as was customary in her native Boston. Her hosts treated her to dinner nearby, then they strolled onto the Seattle Center grounds and settled into the Opera House for the show. The performance was first-rate, a sumptuous classical offering. She was impressed. Equally impressed was a man sitting not far from her. She did not notice him until the performance was over, then she saw him rise, slip a down vest over his plaid shirt, and exit. She smiled. It struck her as the essence of Northwest style: a sunburned outdoorsman coming in from the elements to listen to Mozart.

While many a Seattle native would argue that the backpacker who likes ballet is the homegrown style, long-suffering culture promoters have spent years overcoming a backwoods image. Even while the arts thrive and the city has gained a reputation as one of the nation's best theater towns, even as Seattle continues to bathe in international attention for daring dance shows and original stagings of classic operas, there is a lingering insecurity. It can be traced to a famous broadside by Sir Thomas Beecham, a colorful British conductor who visited Seattle in 1948 at the invitation of citizens who hoped to upgrade the local symphony.

At the time, you could not buy liquor by the drink in any of the bare handful of respectable restaurants. There was no opera, no dance to speak of. Theater was something for the rich to pursue in their spare time. Mark Tobey was on his way to world recognition, but few in the city knew what to make of him and his obsession with the Pike Place Market. Sir Thomas surveyed this arid cultural landscape and said, "If I were a member of the community, I really should get weary of being looked upon as a sort of aesthetic dustbin."

The insult was never forgotten. In the next fifteen years, the cultural climate altered so dramatically that Sir Thomas did not recognize the city on a return visit. For one thing, you could enjoy a cocktail with dinner at the new four-star restaurants that appeared following the change in liquor laws.

Many credit the World's Fair with bringing big league sensibilities and sophistication to the city— or at least a desire for same. In came the Opera House, the Playhouse, the Coliseum, and, in the early 1980s, the Bagley Wright Theatre. Around town, smaller, more risky theaters sprang up and— surprise—most of them survived. Today, the Seattle Repertory Theatre runs second in season ticket-holders to the Seahawks and the Huskies. Off and on, the city has supported almost a dozen equity theaters — more than any city but New York. And that does not count the smaller quality theaters spread around different neighborhoods. In one recent year, three of *Time Magazine's* ten outstanding achievements in theater were linked to Seattle.

The five main professional theaters — the Rep, A Contemporary Theatre, Intiman, Empty Space, Children's — support up to two hundred working actors. Each of the theaters caters to a slightly different crowd, from the traditional to the more avant-garde. The Rep, housed in the new Bagley Wright Theatre, puts six major productions on the boards each season. Among the smaller theaters, the Paul Robeson has conducted several seasons of original productions with ethnic themes, while the Pioneer Square Theater is the home of Seattle's longest running and most successful play — *Angry Housewives*. In a twist that would tweak the sensibilities of Sir Thomas, a staging of the Seattle play was arranged in London in 1986. New theater usually goes the other way. While new stages basked in the spotlights around town, some theater lovers turned their attention to an older institution. The Fifth Avenue Theatre, an acoustically balanced, 2,400-seat house with an ornate interior modeled after the Imperial Palace in Peking's Forbidden City, received a $2.6 million face-lift in 1978—fifty-two years after it first opened. Today, the theater is a home for lavish touring productions.

During this same growth period in the late 1970s, galleries sprouted throughout Pioneer Square. Not one or two, but as many as ten good ones. The situation resembled the old story about the small-town lawyer who had no business until another attorney hung his shingle across the street. Competition — of the genteel, occasionally vicious, artistic type — spurred artists, gallery owners, and buyers. On the one night every month when all the exhibitors unveil their new shows, Pioneer Square is awash with gallery gazers, strolling among sports fans on their way to the Kingdome.

"When I first came here, it struck me that there wasn't a lot going on culturally," recalls an East Coast transplant, who grew up in Manhattan, had an Ivy League education, and lived in Boston before falling in love with Seattle. "It was a little sleepy. But now you can hardly keep up with it all. It's more sophisticated, in every way."

Opera is an example. Until the early 1970s, if you mentioned opera in Seattle most people thought of the Marx Brothers. But with the good acoustics of the Opera House, the willingness on the part of donors to support it, and the unerring good hand of manager Glynn Ross, something was bound to happen. The breakthrough came with the staging of Wagner's *Ring of the Nibelungen* in both English and German. Suddenly, the Seattle Opera Company had itself a summer tourist attraction, as well as music that was accessible to people not normally drawn to the performing arts.

Seattle dance has also leaped to new heights. When the Joffrey Ballet comes to town, the devoted fan knows that Robert Joffrey danced his first steps in Seattle as a boy. But since he has grown up, so has the town. The city's residential company, the Pacific Northwest Ballet, has struggled through some lean years but it has found a home. Its annual Christmas staging of *The Nutcracker* is a crowd-pleaser and as much a part of the holiday season as the December lights atop the Space Needle. In the mid-1980s, the ballet community welcomed back Mark Morris, who grew up in the Mount Baker district, went on to fame in New York, then brought his innovative dance style back home to Seattle and set up a small, residential company.

Another native son, the late Mark Tobey, is one reason the Seattle Art Museum has enjoyed a good international reputation. Tobey, who loved the city during the middle part of the century, studied the faces and moods, the low clouds and men of despair. Even after he moved to Switzerland, Seattle remained part of his art, especially the Pike Place Market. The Art Museum has more than a hundred Tobeys — from the early figurative works on the Market to the later abstract paintings. Museums from around the world have offered exhibits of their national treasures for a chance to show some of Seattle's Tobey collection.

The Art Museum is also home to one of the world's finest collections of Oriental jade. The Asian influence has always been felt in the neighborhoods of Seattle, and the soul-nurturing aspects of Far Eastern culture have been a key to the city's art. At Volunteer Park, Noguchi's double-faced *Black Sun* is a cherished work of outdoor art which seems to express the feelings of Seattle residents toward their source of light and heat.

Outdoor sculptures—in large part the result of a city-financed arts program that has been praised as a national model—have brought warm touches to buildings and parks throughout Seattle. But then, it only seems natural that the lonesome figures depicted in *Waiting for the Interurban*, should blend with the canal view in Fremont, or that Henry Moore's black *Vertebrae* should stop pedestrians on Fourth Avenue. They join older, established figures —the venerable bronze rendering of Chief Sealth in Belltown, the statue of George Washington in the University District— in elevating the urban experience and making Seattle an oasis of art, surrounded by the random sculptings of nature.

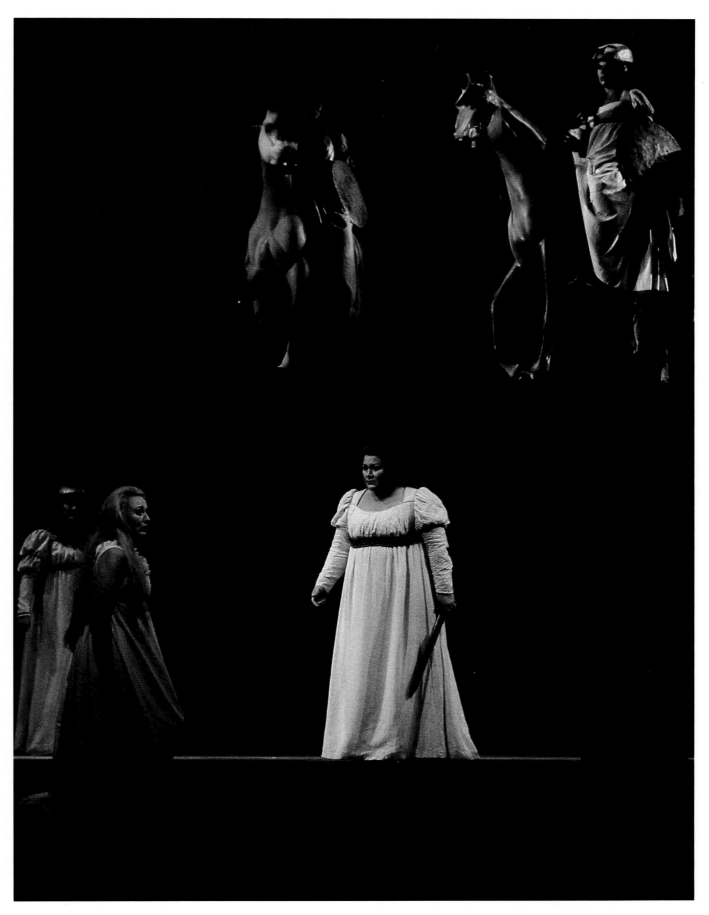

■ *Above:* Brunhild of the Valkyries enchants a Seattle Opera House crowd at a performance of *Die Walküre,* from Wagner's *Ring* cycle. Seattle has received international praise for its annual summer staging of the German classic.

■ *Above:* Noguchi's stirring *Black Sun* in Volunteer Park is also practical—when used as a backrest and a porthole to view the city below.

■ *Above:* Though skeptics said it could not be done, the Pacific Northwest Ballet Company has a healthy following and ambitious future plans.

■ *Above:* The Seattle Repertory Theatre presents Shakespeare's timeless *The Merry Wives of Windsor.* After New York, Seattle is said to be the most active theater town in America.

MOODS OF THE CITY

In some cities, people rarely look up at the sky. Rain or shine, wind or calm, it hardly matters — they stroll through the glass canyons of man until safe under a roof that is usually someone else's floor. Not so in Seattle, a city that never lets the eye rest. During any one day, there may be a dozen different cloud formations, from menacing to harmless, a tease of sunlight one minute, a threat of downpour the next. The clouds open and shut; they rage and disappear. Sometimes they just scoot across a low ceiling, on their way to a collision in the Cascades. What falls from the sky keeps the lakes clean, the gardens fed, and the streets scrubbed. It can soothe a tired soul, or scare a little boy. But whatever form it takes, the sky will never be just background in Seattle.

The first white settlers who landed at Alki Beach looked up at the gray overhead and began to cry. It was raining, a hard November torrent, and they had come to this land expecting a sort of winter paradise. Back in Ohio, they received letters from relatives who had moved to Oregon Country, letters that told of a warm, southerly wind and flowers that blossomed in January. An old sketch shows them huddled with their babies in a lashing storm. A witness wrote that, "Arthur Denny found his wife weeping as she sat on a water-soaked log in the pouring rain."

Three generations later, Brewster Denny sits inside his office at the University of Washington while a storm rages outside. Talking about the city his great-grandfather helped to build, he has some ideas about keeping Seattle's scale human — small enough to remain livable, big enough to satisfy the longings of culture. It's wonderful, he says of the unyielding downpour. "We want to live kindly with the land. We want people who like the rain and think this is paradise."

Some natives go even further in their embrace of the elements. Architect James Olson has studied dark winter days which give way to dashes of pink light just before the curtain of night; he has looked at buildings on diffused days without shade; he has tried to gauge the human mood by this interplay of color and fickle lumination. "I'm convinced we can think better in this misty city," he concludes. "This cloud cover we complain about gives us soft light and a temperate climate."

Many homes in the city reflect this attitude. Views are the rule, rather than the exception. Because of the convergence zone — a term which describes the meeting of southern moisture systems with northern blasts just after they whip around the Olympics and converge on Puget Sound — there may be rain on Queen Anne Hill, while Seward Park is sunny. The hills offer a great perch from which to see these daily changes in sky and light. Homes built in the architectural design known as "Northwest Style" lean out into the weather instead of hiding from it. They are full of wall-sized windows and large patios. Like the smaller, more traditional homes that have punched a hole in the roof and replaced it with a skylight, they reflect a Seattle resident's hunger for light.

Just after a storm is a good time to see the city anew — clean and raw. Evergreens and sun-shy ferns soak in moisture with relish. It is no time to hide. Squirrels emerge from hidden homes to see what the wind has knocked down from the trees. Herons fly low to follow the fish that rise after a rain. Racoons come out from blackberry brambles. Green, the dominant color, is at its best just after a fresh wash from above. Among many reasons, that is one excuse for staring at the sky in Seattle.

■ *Left:* Afternoon light bathes the foremost city of the Pacific Northwest with a golden glow. ■ *Above:* Summer banners along Elliott Way herald the bustling waterfront tourist trade. ■ *Overleaf:* Lake Washington and Puget Sound pinch the hills in the city's bulging midsection.

■ *Above:* While Seattle's pace changes at night, the city is alive with concerts, theater, and other cultural events. ■ *Right:* The city is named for Chief Sealth of the Suquamish, a generous leader who greeted the first white settlers at Alki Beach in 1851.